HIGH INTEREST/LOW READABILITY
NONFICTION

by
Richard Gifford

Cover and Inside Illustrations
Elizabeth Adams

Cover Graphics
Peggy Jackson

Publisher
Instructional Fair • TS Denison
Grand Rapids, Michigan 49544

About the Author

Richard Gifford is a middle school English teacher for learning-disabled students. He holds a Bachelor of Arts in English Literature from the University of Texas and a Master of Arts in Teaching from Johns Hopkins University.

Credits

Author: Richard Gifford
Artist: Elizabeth Adams
Cover Graphics: Peggy Jackson
Text Designer: Pat Geasler
Project Director/Editor: Sharon Kirkwood
Editors: Lisa Hancock, Linda Triemstra

Standard Book Number: 1-56822-824-4
High/Low Nonfiction, Vol. I
Copyright © 1999 by Ideal • Instructional Fair Publishing Group
a division of Tribune Education
2400 Turner Avenue NW
Grand Rapids, Michigan 49544

Table of Contents

Introduction

This book of short articles and activities seeks to stimulate the interests of teenagers who are reading far below their grade level. Teachers who work with this population comment on the scarcity of engaging reading material accessible to these students; this book aims to fill this need. The primary goals of this book are to facilitate ease of readability by means of controlled vocabulary, simple sentence structure, and non-distracting graphic design and to provide interesting articles, relevant to teenage readers whose taste and sophistication are not matched by their ability to read.

The questions and activities were designed according to current educational research on improving the reading comprehension of remedial readers. Adaptability was also a very important consideration when writing this book. The articles, activities, and questions can be used as part of a teacher-directed lesson, or they can be assigned as independent work.

Pre-reading Activities

Looking It Over

1. Read the title of the article that begins on page 6.

2. Leaf through the pages of the article, stopping to look at the illustrations.

3. Read the following list of vocabulary words.

Vocabulary

anaconda   large non-poisonous snake that crushes its prey in coils

Example: The anaconda wrapped around the deer and crushed it.

biologist   person who studies living things

Example: The biologist looked at the cells under a microscope.

Venezuela   country in South America

Example: Lisa needed a passport to go from the United States to Venezuela.

prey   animal hunted for food

Example: Rabbits are the prey of foxes.

Anaconda

unruly	hard to control
	Example: The bear was so unruly it had to be put in a cage by itself.
transmitter	electronic device that sends radio signals
	Example: When the battery died the transmitter stopped sending signals.

Make a Prediction

What do you think this article will be about? Write your prediction and the reason you made it below.

Prediction _____

_____

_____

Reason _____

_____

_____

What do you know?

What do you know about snakes? Make a list of everything you know or *think* you know about snakes. Then read the article to add to your knowledge.

_____

_____

_____

_____

_____

Anaconda

The man takes a step. Mud and muck ooze through his toes. He takes another step. His foot sinks into the soft, squishy bottom of the swamp. The water is too dark and murky to see his feet. He takes another step. This time the swamp mud moves under his bare foot. It's alive. Does he scream in terror and leap 10 feet into the air? No. He smiles. Then he reaches down and pulls up a huge, twisting snake. This is what he does for a living.

Jesús Rivas is a field biologist. He studies the anaconda, which is the largest boa snake that is not poisonous. To study these snakes he must catch them. To catch them he must walk barefoot through swamps in Venezuela.

Rivas is more careful than he used to be. When he was younger, Rivas would put his arm in the water and let the snakes bite him. This way he could find the snake's head so he could catch it. Now Rivas only uses this method when all else fails. For example, he might offer himself as bait if a snake is getting away.

Rivas does not hunt these snakes alone. His research partner is María Muñoz. She is a small woman who wears lipstick and earrings while grabbing anacondas.

Rivas and Muñoz, along with a volunteer or two, have caught over 450 anacondas during their study. The anaconda is known for crushing and eating its prey. However, none of the researchers has suffered more than a bite. There are stories of the anaconda attacking and eating humans, but these stories have not been confirmed.

The main goal of the study is to learn more about the

anaconda's biology. Rivas and Muñoz study the snakes' diets, where they live, and their mating habits. This information will be used to decide if anacondas can be hunted without putting the whole species at risk.

At this time, it is illegal in most South American countries to hunt anacondas. There is not a very big market for the snakes anyway. Their dark skins do not make flashy belts or boots. Also, the anaconda is too unruly to be a good pet. The biggest threat to the snake is ranchers. They often kill anacondas on sight.

When female anacondas are ready to mate they give off a scent. Males pick up this scent with their tongues and come from long distances. Anacondas learn a lot about their environment through their tongues. Rivas puts it this way, "Their flicking tongues give them a whole universe we aren't aware of."

Muñoz and Rivas use this trait to help them catch the snakes. They find a female ready to mate and just wait for the males to show up. When the researchers have collected a load of anacondas they take them back to their

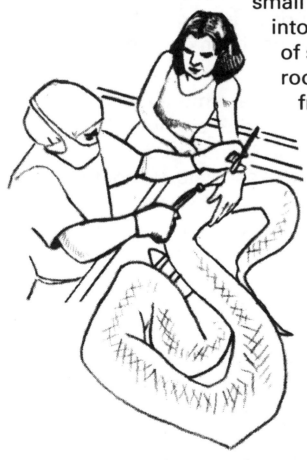

small house. The snakes are put into old sacks. These sacks full of snakes lay all over the living room floor. Sometimes Muñoz freaks out when the sacks start moving around at night.

An old sock serves as an important research tool for Muñoz and Rivas. When they are ready to study a snake they pull it from a sack. Then they slip a sock over the snake's head and wrap it with tape. The sock blinds the snake and calms it down. It also stops the snake from biting.

The researchers measure the anacondas. There are reports of anacondas over 30 feet long. So far the longest snake Muñoz and Rivas have found was 17 feet long. The heaviest snake weighed 215 pounds. The females are usually larger than the males.

The researchers also record the date, hour, and location of the find. Then they mark the snake and take a blood sample. Sometimes Rivas will implant a transmitter in a snake to help track it.

Muñoz and Rivas have been studying the giant snakes for more than five years. However, they don't need to worry about the work becoming boring. When Muñoz and Rivas are not being bitten, they keep making surprising new discoveries. For example, they found that when a female anaconda is pregnant, she will not eat for six to eight months. Muñoz and Rivas were keeping a pregnant anaconda to observe. They were worried that the snake was starving itself to death. After the female gave birth, she had a little snack—seven ducks and chickens!

Comprehension

Circle the best answer. Highlight the sentence or sentences in the story where you find each answer.

1. Jesús Rivas finds anacondas by . . .

   a. spotting them through a telescope.

   b. walking barefoot through a swamp.

   c. looking under logs.

   d. looking in trees.

2. When Rivas was younger, he caught snakes . . .

   a. with a net.

   b. with a rope.

   c. with a trap.

   d. by letting the snakes bite him on the arm.

3. While catching snakes, Maria Muñoz wears . . .

   a. lipstick and earrings.

   b. gloves.

   c. body armor.

   d. a helmet.

4. During their study, the anacondas caught by Rivas and Muñoz have numbered . . .

   a. 500.

   b. less than 30.

   c. 275.

   d. more than 450.

5. The main goal of the study is to . . .

   a. kill anacondas.

   b. learn more about the anaconda's biology.

   c. catch as many snakes as possible.

   d. none of the above.

6. The market for anacondas is small because . . .

   a. their skins don't make flashy boots and belts.

   b. they die at a young age.

   c. they are not good pets.

   d. a and c.

7. The biggest threat to the anaconda is . . .

   a. ranchers who kill them on sight.

   b. other anacondas.

   c. pollution.

   d. monkeys.

8. When female anacondas are ready to mate they . . .

   a. change colors.

   b. shed their skins.

   c. give off a scent.

   d. all of the above.

9. Researchers calm the snakes . . .

   a. with drugs.

   b. by rubbing the snake's belly.

   c. by putting a sock over the snake's head.

   d. with all of the above.

10. When a female anaconda is pregnant she will . . .

    a. not eat for 6-8 months.

    b. build a nest in a cave.

    c. hunt all day and night.

    d. go to sleep for 6-8 months.

Find the Adjectives

An adjective is a word used to describe a noun or a pronoun. Find and circle the adjective in each row.

1.	mud	soft	step
2.	squishy	foot	scream
3.	huge	this	leap
4.	move	time	dark
5.	hunt	young	Maria
6.	small	grab	with
7.	we	big	pick
8.	this	trait	flashy
9.	unruly	just	snake
10.	over	small	find

Extension Activity

Catching an anaconda with your bare hands doesn't sound like such a good idea. Design a trap you might use to catch an anaconda. You can describe the trap in a couple of paragraphs or draw a picture of it. If you draw a picture, write some short descriptions.

Name _____

Pre-reading Activities

Looking It Over

1. Read the title of the article that begins on page 15.

2. Leaf through the pages of the article, stopping to look at the illustrations.

3. Read the following list of vocabulary words.

Vocabulary

engraving   picture that has been carved into a flat surface

Example: Tina carved an engraving of a hawk on a piece of oak.

lofty   to be high up, towering

Example: The owl watched the mouse from a lofty branch in the tree.

mutiny   to rebel against a leader

Example: There was a mutiny on the ship when the crew refused to follow the captain's orders.

pentagon   a five-sided shape

Example: Jose made a birdhouse in the shape of a pentagon.

13

Name _____

perch   a place for resting or sitting

> **Example:** The wide spot on the cliff made a nice perch for looking down into the valley.

tepee   cone-shaped shelter

> **Example:** The tepee has been used for shelter by Native Americans for hundreds of years.

Make a Prediction

What do you think this story will be about? Write your prediction and the reason you made it below.

Prediction _____

_____

_____

Reason _____

_____

_____

What do you know?

What do you know about tree houses? Make a list of everything you know or *think* you know about tree houses. Then read the article to add to your knowledge.

_____

_____

_____

Tree Houses Grow Up

When most people think of tree houses, they think of kids in the backyard with a few scraps of wood, some rusty nails, and a couple of old hammers. When the house is finished, the walls lean like the Tower of Pisa. The floor is full of splinters. The roof, if there is one, leaks. After all, the house is only for play. No one would ever live there. Well, think again, because tree houses aren't just for kids anymore.

Today, adults are getting in on the tree-house action. They are building houses among the birds to use as offices, vacation homes, and even to live in full-time. People are writing books and teaching classes on how to build houses in the trees. There are even companies that sell portable tree houses.

There is almost no limit to the uses adults find for these buildings in the branches. Albert Green built a two-room cottage in a giant pine tree on his Montana ranch. From this lofty perch he watches deer and elk below. They don't even know he's there. In Washington State two other men built a tree cabin in the shape of a pentagon. They installed a stereo and a TV. The cabin also includes two bunks that fold out, a trap door, and a golf tee on the roof! Another man built his house 90 feet up in a poplar tree. His dog rides up in a rope-and-barrel elevator.

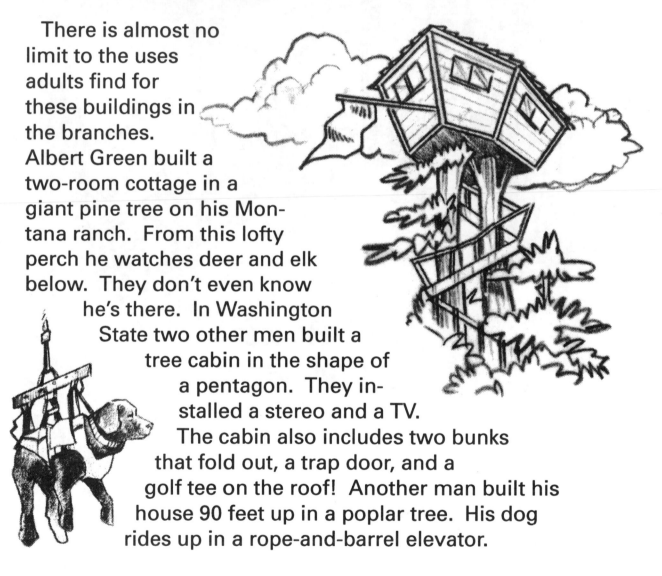

One man leading this rush to the trees is Peter Nelson. He has been called "Mr. Tree House." In the past few years, Nelson has built over a dozen tree houses. He even wrote a book on the subject. He built one house in Japan to be used as a campsite. Nelson built another in Clam Gulch, Alaska. It cost only about $2,000 and took eight days to build. It is set in four spruce trees. The house includes a small deck with railing, large bay windows, and pine paneling. The owner describes it as "a work of art."

History tells us that adults building shelters in trees is nothing new. Old engravings from the South Pacific show people living in "nests." It seems they rode up and down in baskets. In New Guinea, tree houses provided safety from invaders. Some people in New Guinea still live in tree houses made out of palm fronds. In France, two chapels were built in oak trees over 300 years ago. The chapels have survived lightning strikes and stand to this day.

Perhaps the most unusual tree house is built by a Canadian company. You can take it with you. This portable tree house has two stories and is shaped like a tepee. It takes about six hours to put up. The first floor has a three-burner stove and a sink. A ladder leads to the bedroom on the second floor. The roof can be zipped open so you can sleep under the stars.

One happy customer is forester Ron Adair. Adair and his crew work deep in the Canadian forest. Sometimes they have to be flown in by helicopter. They used to camp out in tents. Now they camp out in the trees.   Adair's crew call their portable tree house "Bush Condo."

For the foresters, setting up camp in the trees is not just fun and games. They have good reason to want to get off the ground. Bears! Huge grizzlies come into camp looking for food. Most of the time the foresters can scare them away by banging on pots and pans.

However, sometimes the bears will not give up. Then the cook has to take it to the next level: "bear grenades." A bear grenade is a can of mace wrapped in bacon. One bite out of this treat usually does the trick.

Adair and his crew love their house in a tree. If he, as their leader, even talked about going back to the old tents, Adair says, "I'd have a mutiny on my hands."

Comprehension

Circle the best answer. Highlight the sentence or sentences in the story where you find the answer.

1. Adults are building tree houses to . . .
   a. live in full time.
   b. use as vacation homes.
   c. use as offices.
   d. all of the above.

2. Albert Green used his tree house for . . .
   a. watching for fires.
   b. star gazing.
   c. watching deer and elk.
   d. an office.

3. A tree cabin in Washington State includes . . .
   a. a shower.
   b. a stereo.
   c. a golf tee.
   d. b and c.

4. Peter Nelson is . . .
   a. a builder of tree houses.
   b. a forester.
   c. a rancher.
   d. none of the above.

5. The house Peter Nelson built in Alaska cost . . .
   a. $30,000.
   b. $100.
   c. $10,000.
   d. $2,000.

6. Adults have been building tree houses for . . .

   a. at least 300 years.

   b. 5 years.

   c. about 100 years.

   d. 50 years.

7. Old engravings from the South Pacific show people . . .

   a. hunting from trees.

   b. living in nests.

   c. fishing from trees.

   d. a and c.

8. Two 300-year-old French chapels have survived . . .

   a. earthquakes.

   b. lightning.

   c. fire.

   d. floods.

9. The portable tree house built by a Canadian company . . .

   a. is shaped like a tepee.

   b. has two stories.

   c. has a zipper in the roof.

   d. all of the above.

10. The foresters scare away bears . . .

   a. by banging on pots and pans.

   b. with cans of mace wrapped in bacon.

   c. a and b.

   d. by shooting them.

Find the Verbs

A verb is an action word. It describes what people or things do. Find and circle the verb in each row.

1.   kid   tree   grow
2.   think   house   wood
3.   of   build   men
4.   class   sell   rope
5.   one   only   watch
6.   put   action   there
7.   stove   tell   new
8.   bang   most   happy
9.   look   animal   hot
10. crew   sleep   chapel

Extension Activity

Design your own tree house on paper. As you create your design, think about how you want to use the tree house. Think about what features you would want to include. Think about how it will fit in the tree. When you finish, share your design with your class.

Pre-reading Activities

Looking It Over

1. Read the title of the article that begins on page 24.

2. Leaf through the pages of the article, stopping to look at the illustration.

3. Read the following list of vocabulary words.

Vocabulary

scent   an odor or smell

   Example: A skunk has a very strong scent.

canine   relating to dogs; dog-like

   Example: The big white poodle was Bob's canine friend.

bacteria   one-cell organisms that often cause disease

   Example: When meat sits out on the counter, bacteria grows on it.

praise   a compliment

   Example: The teacher gave Nina a lot of praise when she earned an *A* on her math test.

veteran	person who has a lot of experience in a job or activity
	Example: The veteran carpenter had been building houses for 50 years.
rubble	pieces of rock
	Example: After the landslide, rubble blocked the road.

Make a Prediction

What do you think this article will be about? Write your prediction and the reason you made it below.

Prediction _____

_____

_____

Reason _____

_____

_____

What do you know?

What do you know about search-and-rescue dogs? Make a list of everything you know or *think* you know about search-and-rescue dogs. Then read the article to add to your knowledge.

_____

_____

_____

_____

Bring 'Em Back Alive

At 3:00 A.M. the mountain air was cold. Jazz's wet nose was cold. Kendra's trail was cold—8 hours cold. That was going to make it harder for Jazz to find her. After such a long time Kendra's scent would not be easy to pick up and follow.

Twelve-year-old Kendra was hiking with her dog in the mountains of Colorado when she lost her way. She panicked and for a while she ran screaming through the woods. Finally, Kendra calmed down. Her dog was still with her. She sat down at the edge of a field of boulders and held her dog for warmth.

The sheriff's department and some campers had spent hours looking for Kendra. Now it was Jazz's turn. His owner, Wendy Wampler, led Jazz to the point where Kendra was last seen. Jazz took off and Wendy followed. Just before dawn, Wendy called out for Kendra and then heard someone call back. Jazz had found Kendra. She was cold and wet, but alive. Later, Kendra and her parents named their new puppy Jazz in honor of the canine hero.

Search-and-rescue dogs such as Jazz are not born heroes. It can take months of intense training for a dog and its owner to master the skills needed to find a person who is lost in the woods. Dogs learn to find people buried under tons of snow, or trapped in collapsed buildings, or even dead.

To learn these skills, the dog and owner go to school. At search-and-rescue school the dogs learn to pick up a scent and follow it. They learn how to climb ladders, ride ski lifts, and move safely through disaster sites. They learn how to tell their owners they have found someone.

For the owners, this training is very serious. A person's life may depend on it. For the dogs, the training is fun and games. And the first game many of them learn is hide-and-seek.

Tasha is just starting her training. At this point, she is not even in school yet. Tasha's owner, Sue Purvis, takes Tasha into the woods. Tasha is held back by a friend and Purvis runs off into the woods. Tasha is told, "Go find her." She does. The game gets harder. Tasha has to find the friend next. Then she has to find Purvis without being able to see which direction she went. After that, Tasha doesn't get to see the person she is looking for. She has to pick up the scent from a piece of the person's clothing. When Tasha does well she gets lots of praise. She also gets to play with a favorite toy.

Not all dogs are cut out for search and rescue. Veteran trainers talk about the "bunny issue." One trainer put it this way, "If your dog chases rabbits and doesn't come right off it when called, you may not have a search dog."

Another trainer warned that no matter how much training some dogs get, they still "can't find a hamburger in a phone booth."

How do dogs "find hamburger in a phone booth" or a person buried under pounds of rubble? A dog's sense of smell is highly developed. It is probably 1,000 to 10,000 times keener than a human's. Dogs see the world with their nose. Giving a dog a scent to follow is like showing it a picture.

People give dogs a very clear picture to follow in the form of dead skin cells. Every minute humans shed tens of thousands of dead skin cells. As the skin cells and sweat are broken down by bacteria, they give off a gas. The gas is like an invisible trail that dogs can follow on the ground and in the air. Dogs can even smell the gas through water, snow, mud, and concrete.

Cassidy, a big white poodle, plows through the snow. Two people are buried five feet under the surface. She has to find them fast, before they smother or freeze to death. Cassidy runs straight to a spot over one of the bodies and begins digging. Her trainer asks, "Where's the other one?" She flies across the snow and begins digging again. She finds both people in minutes. It would have taken a human search-and-rescue team over 30 hours to do the same job. By that time, both people could have been dead. Today it was training, only fun and games. Tomorrow, it might mean life or death.

Name _____

Comprehension

Circle the best answer. Highlight the sentence or sentences in the story where you find the answer.

1. When Kendra became lost, she was hiking in . . .

    a. the Colorado mountains.

    b. Montana.

    c. the Arizona desert.

    d. the Texas hill country.

2. Jazz found Kendra by . . .

    a. spotting her red coat.

    b. hearing her screams.

    c. following her scent.

    d. running in circles.

3. To master search-and-rescue skills, a dog must train . . .

    a. hours.

    b. weeks.

    c. months.

    d. none of the above.

4. At search-and-rescue school dogs learn to . . .

    a. follow a scent.

    b. tell their owners they have found someone.

    c. move safely through disaster sites.

    d. all of the above.

5. One of the first games dogs learn during training is to . . .

    a. fetch.

    b. roll over.

    c. play dead.

    d. play hide-and-seek.

6. When Tasha does well at hide-and-seek, she . . .

   a. is praised.

   b. gets to play with a toy.

   c. gets a snack.

   d. a and b.

7. The "bunny issue" exists when . . .

   a. a dog won't chase rabbits.

   b. a dog is scared of rabbits.

   c. a dog chases rabbits and won't come back.

   d. none of the above.

8. A dog's sense of smell is _____ times better than a human's.

   a. 1,000 to 10,000

   b. 3 to 5

   c. 10,000 to 100,000

   d. 100 to 1,000

9. When finding humans, dogs follow a trail created by . . .

   a. foot prints.

   b. dead skin cells.

   c. bread crumbs.

   d. torn clothing.

10. It would take a human search-and-rescue team _____ to find the people Cassidy found in minutes.

   a. 1 hour

   b. 2 weeks

   c. over 30 hours

   d. 15 hours

Find the Nouns

A noun is the name of a person, place, or thing. Find and circle the nouns in each row.

1.   poodle   run   big

2.   bury   sleep   snow

3.   body   dig   them

4.   by   trainer   and

5.   job   might   find

6.   fly   game   hit

7.   in   puppy   over

8.   favorite   trapped   hero

9.   bunny   give   off

10.   skin   are   how

Extension Activity

What should you do if you are lost in the wilderness? Find out. Call the offices of a state or national park in your area. Ask if they can send some information on things to do when you get lost. Ask if they know of any trainers of search-and-rescue dogs in your area who could visit your school.

Name _____

Pre-reading Activities

Looking It Over

1. Read the title of the article that begins on page 32.

2. Leaf through the pages of the article, stopping to look at the illustrations.

3. Read the following list of vocabulary words.

Vocabulary

Anasazi ancestors of modern Pueblo Indians

Example: The Anasazi lived in the American Southwest hundreds of years ago.

drought a long period with little or no rain

Example: The drought caused all of the crops to die.

evidence data that support a belief or judgment

Example: You must have evidence that someone has committed a crime before you can arrest that person.

fortress a building that protects people from attack

Example: The enemy could not break through the strong walls of the fortress.

theory   a belief supported by evidence

> **Example:** There can be more than one theory based on the same set of evidence.

Make a Prediction

What do you think this story will be about? Write your prediction and the reason you made it below.

Prediction _____

_____

_____

Reason _____

_____

_____

What do you know?

What do you know about the Pueblo Indians? Make a list of everything you know or *think* you know about the Pueblos. Then read the article to add to your knowledge.

_____

_____

_____

_____

_____

The Enemy Within

In the desert of the southwest United States you can find huge buildings made of stone and mud that are more than 1,000 years old. They are still standing after all these years, like ancient apartments whose tenants have vanished. Who built these buildings? Why did they leave them? Where did they go? Today, scientists are trying to find the answers to these questions. They want to solve the mystery of the "Old Ones."

The Old Ones is what some modern Pueblo Indians call their ancestors. They are also known as the Anasazi. The Anasazi lived in what is now Arizona, New Mexico, Colorado, and Utah. They lived there long before the United States even existed.

The Anasazi constructed buildings out of a mixture of mud and sandstone. The buildings, which often contained hundreds of rooms, were sometimes more than five stories high. Special rooms were built to hold corn, beans, and other foods. Wooden ladders were used to connect the many levels.

At one time, there were over 150 Anasazi villages spread across the Southwest. They were linked by a system of roads at least 200 miles long. The villages were usually located in valleys, close to crops and water. Scientists think that the Anasazi lived peacefully in these villages for hundreds of years. But then something happened that drove the Anasazi out of their peaceful villages and into fortresses high up on cliffs.

About 700 hundred years ago the Anasazi began building cliff dwellings. Their new mud and stone "apartments" were built on cliffs hundreds of feet above their

old villages. This puzzled many scientists. Why would the Anasazi move farther away from water and their crops down in the valleys? Life would be much harder up in the cliff villages.

Only one answer made sense. The Anasazi moved up onto the cliffs because they were under attack from an enemy. Villages on cliffs would be easier to defend. Other evidence supports this theory. The Anasazi began to build walls and watchtowers. Skeletons have been found that show marks of attack. But who was the enemy?

Some scientists used to believe that the Anasazi were attacked by other tribes, such as the Navajo or the Utes. Other scientists disagreed. They said there was no evidence that these tribes had been in the area. Now scientists have a new theory. The Anasazi's enemies were other Anasazi.

Life in the desert is hard. There is not much water. It takes a lot of work to raise food. Some scientists think that a drought made life much harder for the Anasazi. Their crops died. There was not enough food. So the Anasazi began to attack each other to survive. And for protection they began to build villages in the sky.

The mystery of the Old Ones does not end there. Less than 50 years after the Anasazi built the villages on the cliffs, they moved again. This time they left the area where they had lived for thousands of years. The Anasazi began moving to the south and the east.

No one knows why the Anasazi left the land where they had lived for so long. However, scientists have an interesting theory. The Pueblo Indians started a new religion around the same time the Anasazi left their old homes. The Pueblos held dances where they wore masks and asked the spirits, or "kachinas," for good crops, health, and happiness. Some scientists think the Anasazi moved to join this new religion.

Today, many Pueblos still practice the kachina religion. And they tell stories of the Old Ones who left their homes hundreds of years ago.

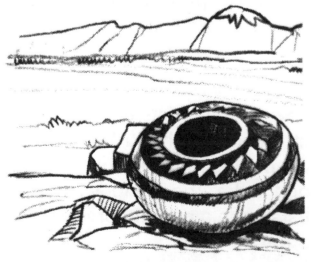

Comprehension

Circle the best answer. Highlight the sentence or sentences in the story where you find the answer.

1. The ancestors of the Pueblo Indians were the . . .

   a. Ute.

   b. Navajo.

   c. Anasazi.

   d. Sioux.

2. The Anasazi's buildings were made of . . .

   a. brick.

   b. sticks.

   c. buffalo hides.

   d. mud and stone.

3. The Anasazi lived in the deserts of the . . .

   a. Southwest.

   b. Northeast.

   c. Northwest.

   d. Midwest.

4. The Anasazi villages were linked by . . .

   a. rivers.

   b. roads.

   c. railroad tracks.

   d. none of the above.

5. For hundreds of years, Anasazi villages were located _____ , close to water and crops.

   a. in the mountains

   b. in valleys

   c. on cliffs

   d. near the plains

6. One theory says the Anasazi began to build on cliffs because . . .

   a. they liked the view.

   b. it was easier to collect rainwater.

   c. it was too crowded in the valleys.

   d. they were under attack.

7. The latest theory says that the Anasazi were attacked by . . .

   a. other Anasazi.

   b. the Utes.

   c. the Navajo.

   d. none of the above.

8. The Anasazi lived in their cliff villages for . . .

   a. about 100 years.

   b. about 300 years.

   c. more than 400 years.

   d. less than 50 years.

9. The Anasazi might have left the area where they had lived for thousands of years . . .

   a. to look for jobs.

   b. to join a new religion.

   c. because they were bored.

   d. to get away from evil spirits.

10. Today, the Pueblos still . . .

    a. practice the kachina religion.

    b. tell stories about the Anasazi.

    c. a and b.

    d. none of the above.

Name _____

Theory and Evidence

Match each set of evidence to the correct theory.

Theory	**Evidence**

_____ The Anasazi were under attack.

_____ The Anasazi moved to join the Pueblo Indians' new religion.

a. The Anasazi built villages on cliffs.

b. The Pueblo tell stories about the Anasazi.

c. Skeletons have been found with marks of attack.

d. The Anasazi built walls and watchtowers.

e. The Anasazi moved to the south and east.

f. The Pueblo Indians started a new religion around the same time the Anasazi left their old homes.

Extension Activity

In small groups of three or four, visit the library to find information on the Anasazi. Ask the librarian to help you locate books on the Anasazi. Look up Anasazi in an encyclopedia. Find at least three facts about the Anasazi and report them to your class.

Pre-reading Activities

Looking It Over

1. Read the title of the article that begins on page 40.

2. Leaf through the pages of the article, stopping to look at the illustrations.

3. Read the following list of vocabulary words.

Vocabulary

cataract a dark film that grows on the eye and causes blindness

Example: The dog kept bumping into walls after he developed cataracts.

cornea tough, clear covering of the eye

Example: When sand got in Rob's eye it scratched his cornea.

iguana large tropical lizard

Example: The iguana is bigger than most lizards.

rodent small mammals often considered pests

Example: Susan put out traps to catch the rodents in her house.

veterinarian doctor who treats animals

Example: The veterinarian had to put a muzzle on the dog before she gave it a shot.

asthma   a disease that makes it hard for a
                   person to breathe

                   Example: Maria's older brother suffers
                   from asthma.

Make a Prediction

What do you think this article will be about? Write your
prediction and the reason you made it below.

Prediction _____

_____

_____

Reason _____

_____

_____

What do you know?

What do you know about veterinarians? Make a list of
everything you know or *think* you know about veterinarians. Then read the article to add to your knowledge.

_____

_____

_____

_____

_____

Animal Hospital

At first glance this hospital looks like many other big-city hospitals. Busy doctors hurry down the halls. Patients with gunshot wounds and knife cuts lay on tables. People sit in the waiting room wondering if their loved ones will be o.k.

But wait a second. A closer look reveals something a little different about this hospital. That IV bag is hooked up to a dog. In an operating room a mouse is x-rayed before surgery. A cat comes in to get a CAT scan.

This is no ordinary hospital. This is the Animal Medical Center (AMC) in New York City. AMC is one of the largest and busiest animal hospitals in the world. It is open 24 hours a day and treats over 65,000 animals each year. AMC cares for a wide variety of animals. Tigers visit from the Bronx Zoo. Dogs come in from around the corner. Pets are flown in from across the globe. One doctor says, "If you stick around here long enough you will see just about every creature on the planet smaller than a cow."

The doctor looks into Mushka's eye with a microscope. She cuts open the dog's cornea and lens. The lens is covered with a cataract which blinds Mushka. An ultrasound probe is used to break up the lens; a vacuum sucks it out. The doctor replaces the old lens with an artificial one. She sews up the eye. This complex surgery is common at AMC.

The hospital was founded in 1910. Its goal was to provide medical care to New York's ill and injured animals. At that time most animals were considered workers, not pets. Cats chased mice. Dogs guarded flocks of sheep.

As the city grew, attitudes changed. Farms were replaced by houses and apartments. Animals moved inside and became members of the family. There is another big difference between the hospital in 1910 and today. Back then most of the veterinarians were men. Now over two-thirds of the graduates from veterinary school are women.

Sylvia, the mouse, is getting an x-ray. Next, she is shaved for surgery and hooked to an instrument to monitor her heart. Operating on animals as small as mice can be tricky. No tube can be inserted to help the mouse breathe. The area for operation is very small. While the pet may be tiny, the owner's love for Sylvia is huge. She has told the vets to do whatever it takes to heal the mouse.

A doctor wanders in to watch the operation. He comments that half the people are killing rodents while the other half bring them to the hospital. Some people do both at the same time. Someone once brought in their pet rat. It had eaten the poison put out for the wild rats and mice.

Something is wrong with Fingers, an iguana. He is a sickly yellow and orange color. He should be green with brown and black streaks. The problem may be Fingers's diet. What does the lizard eat? "Vegetables, nails, and screws," says the vet. "He has free run of the house. We think there's a quarter in there, a screw, and I don't know what else."

Fingers is cut open, and the vet pulls out a quarter, a nickel, and a penny. The screw that was spotted in an x-ray four years earlier is gone. Fingers must have passed it. Ouch!!!

Many of the pets that come to AMC pass through the emergency room. Just as with human hospitals, the emergency room is for patients who need immediate care. One dog came in with stomach pains after gobbling up a chocolate cake. The problem was not too much cake. It was the 12-inch knife that had been used to cut the cake. The knife was removed in surgery and the dog survived.

Another vet examines a kitten. It had been dropped four stories, but it does not seem to be badly hurt. During the summer, AMC staff see a flood of these cases. Cats jump or fall out of open windows from high-rise apartments. Once a cat fell 46 stories and lived. That was a record for the hospital.

On a nearby table another vet tries to save the life of a dog hit by a bus. Waiting in line are a cat with asthma, a dog with seizures, and another dog that is vomiting. One of the vets is on her way to a human hospital with a bite from an ungrateful patient. Just another day at the AMC.

Name _____

Comprehension

Circle the best answer. Highlight the sentence or sentences in the story where you find the answer.

1. The Animal Medical Center is located in . . .
    a. Berlin.
    b. Los Angeles.
    c. Houston.
    d. New York City.

2. The number of animals the Animal Medical Center treats each year is . . .
    a. less than 3,000.
    b. more than 65,000.
    c. more than 100,000.
    d. none of the above.

3. At the Animal Medical Center, vets treat . . .
    a. only cats and dogs.
    b. people.
    c. a wide variety of animals.
    d. only pets.

4. Mushka was having an operation on her eye because she . . .
    a. had cataracts.
    b. had been shot in the eye.
    c. had been in a dog fight.
    d. had been scratched by a cat.

5. When the Animal Medical Center was founded in 1910 . . .
    a. most animals were workers, not pets.
    b. most veterinarians were men.
    c. animals were more healthy than they are today.
    d. a and b.

6. Today, two-thirds of the graduates of veterinary schools are . . .

   a. rich.

   b. women.

   c. men.

   d. from New York.

7. It is hard to operate on mice because they . . .

   a. are so mean.

   b. are so small.

   c. run away.

   d. a and c.

8. Fingers the iguana needed surgery because he had . . .

   a. eaten coins.

   b. broken his leg.

   c. eaten a big cake.

   d. asthma.

9. A dog came to the emergency room with stomach pains because he had eaten . . .

   a. a knife.

   b. too much cake.

   c. nails and screws.

   d. all of the above.

10. A lot of cats come to the Animal Medical Center during the summer because they . . .

   a. suffer heat stroke.

   b. catch the flu.

   c. get into fights.

   d. fall from open windows.

Animals We Love

Some pets become almost like members of the family. Have you ever had a special pet? Is there one type of animal you really like? Use the space below to write about your favorite pet or animal.

_____

_____

_____

_____

_____

_____

_____

_____

_____

Extension Activity

Do animals and humans get the same diseases? How does medical treatment for animals differ from treatment for humans? What is the most dangerous animal for a vet to treat? These are some questions you might ask a vet. Invite a veterinarian to speak to your class or ask if you can conduct an interview over the phone. The class should come up with a list of questions before the visit or interview.

Pre-reading Activities

Looking It Over

1. Read the title of the article that begins on page 48.

2. Leaf through the pages of the article, stopping to look at the illustrations.

3. Read the following list of vocabulary words.

Vocabulary

colonist   person who settles in a land set aside for new settlement

Example: The colonists chopped down all of the trees so they could plant crops.

suspense   wondering what will happen next

Example: The teacher kept the students in suspense until Monday morning.

deserter   person who runs away from the military

Example: During WW II, deserters from the German army hid in barns and basements.

cargo   the goods carried on a ship

Example: All of the cargo was lost when the ship sank.

patrol   a military group that is sent out to
                      explore an area

                      Example: When the patrol spotted the
                      enemy they reported it.

ember   piece of slowly burning coal or wood

                      Example: The ember was red hot, but
                      there was no flame.

Make a Prediction

What do you think this story will be about? Write your
prediction and the reason you made it below.

Prediction _____

_____

_____

Reason _____

_____

_____

What do you know?

What do you know about shipwrecks? Make a list of
everything you know or *think* you know about them.
Then read the article to add to your knowledge.

_____

_____

_____

_____

_____

Shipwrecked

In the winter of 1685, Robert La Salle, a French explorer, sailed into Matagorda Bay on the coast of Texas. He would never sail out. La Salle had made a big mistake. He thought the Mississippi River flowed into the bay.

This was just one of many mistakes in a story with as much horror, suspense, and action as any Hollywood movie. The story's last chapter would be pulled from the muddy bottom of Matagorda Bay 300 years later.

On an earlier trip, La Salle had sailed down the Mississippi River. At that time he claimed most of North America for France. He named it Louisiana, in honor of Louis XIV, the French king. However, there was a problem. Spain was already in the area. In fact, the Spanish had arrived over 100 years earlier.

La Salle came up with a secret plan. He would return with soldiers and colonists. This time they planned to sail *up* the Mississippi and build a fort. Then they would recruit 15,000 Indians to help them attack Spanish forts and silver mines. France would then lay claim to much of North America.

La Salle put his plan into action. In 1684, he set sail for the New World with four ships and 300 men, women, and children. Almost from the very beginning things began to go wrong. One of the ships was captured by the Spanish near Haiti. La Salle and 50 others became ill. Men began to desert. Since some of the deserters were picked up by the Spanish, La Salle's plan to invade through the Gulf of Mexico was discovered. Years before the Spanish had declared the Gulf off-limits. The penalty for trespassing was death.

La Salle continued with his plan. He landed near what is today Galveston, Texas. La Salle made contact with the local Karankawa Indians. During one of their meetings, the Karankawas captured a few of his men. La Salle was on his way to get the men back when he heard a cannon shot from one of his ships. The ship had hit a sandbar and was sinking. For days the crew tried to save the ship and its cargo, but it sank along with most of the goods on board.

This setback didn't stop La Salle. He sent one of his ships back to France. The remaining ship was called the *Belle.* La Salle sailed the *Belle* into Matagorda Bay. On the banks of a small creek, he built his fort. During this time many of his crew and colonists died from overwork, illness, snake bites, and Karankawan arrows. La Salle and twenty of his men set out to explore the area. Before leaving, he ordered his crew to stay on board the *Belle* until he returned in 10 days. This order led to disaster.

La Salle did not return for three months. Men began dying of thirst because the crew had run out of fresh water. A fierce storm hit. The crew was weak. There were not enough men left to sail the ship properly. The *Belle* ran aground and sank.

Any hope for La Salle's mission sank with the *Belle.* As he continued to explore the area, he realized that he was nowhere near the Mississippi. By early 1687, there were only 40 survivors left. La Salle came up with a new plan. He and 17 of his men would travel on foot to a French fort 3,000 miles to the north. From there they hoped to get a message to France to send a rescue ship. This plan also failed.

During the trip some of his men rebelled. They killed La Salle and three others. Then the rebels began fighting each other.

The fighting ended when the last two killers shot each other at the same time and died. When all the killing was over six survivors continued their journey.

On the way they left one boy, Pierre Talon, with a tribe called the Hasinai. Pierre was supposed to make friends with the tribe so they would help the French.

Back at the fort, the Karankawas attacked. All of the colonists were killed except for five children. They were saved by Indian women. The women took them into the tribe to be raised as Karankawas. One of the boys was Jean-Baptiste Talon, brother of Pierre.

Years later both brothers were captured by different Spanish patrols. They came together again in Mexico City. The brothers were forced to serve in the Spanish navy. Their ship was captured by the French near Cuba. Thirteen years after La Salle had left France, the last survivors of his secret mission came home.

This was the end of the story—until 300 years later. In July of 1995, Barto Arnold, a marine scientist, ended his 17-year search for the *Belle.* He saw little blips on the screen of his high-tech metal detector. Arnold sent divers down to check it out. When the team found one of the *Belle's* cannons, they knew they had struck the jackpot.

Normally, a wreck like the *Belle* would be recovered by divers, but the scientists had another idea. They built a massive wall around the ship. Next they pumped out all of the saltwater. Then the research team put down boards so they could lie on top of the mud. Finally, they carefully pulled and scraped the *Belle's* secrets out of the muck.

The mud had kept the ship's wood well preserved. However, as soon as the wood was exposed to the air it began to dissolve. The team had to keep the wood wet and covered. One team member described it this way, "Every thing is on fire. All we can do is try to slow it down to coals and embers."

The *Belle* has been called the most important shipwreck ever found in North America. The list of goods recovered from the site is amazing: three cannons, brass pots, wood combs, glass beads, rings, candlesticks, rifles, and a skeleton. The team even found the bones of one of La Salle's crew. The man had curled up 300 years ago in a coil of rope and died. His role in this amazing tale of adventure and disaster was over. Until now.

Comprehension

Circle the best answer. Highlight the sentence or sentences in the story where you find the answer.

1. La Salle began his plan in the year . . .

    a. A.D. 300.

    b. 1864.

    c. 1684.

    d. 1687.

2. La Salle claimed most of North America for . . .

    a. France.

    b. Germany.

    c. England.

    d. Spain.

3. La Salle's secret plan was to . . .

    a. kidnap the king of Spain.

    b. attack Cuba.

    c. spy on England.

    d. build a fort and attack Spanish mines and forts.

4. One of La Salle's ships was captured by the Spanish . . .

    a. off the coast of Haiti.

    b. off the coast of Texas.

    c. after a long battle.

    d. none of the above.

5. After landing on the Texas coast, La Salle made contact with . . .

    a. the French.

    b. Karankawa Indians.

    c. the English.

    d. runaway slaves.

6. One of La Salle's ships sank after . . .

   a. hitting a reef.

   b. getting shot by a cannon ball.

   c. hitting a sandbar.

   d. none of the above.

7. La Salle built his fort . . .

   a. on the banks of the Mississippi.

   b. in Florida.

   c. next to a big lake.

   d. on the banks of a small creek.

8. La Salle and his men tried to reach a French fort to the north . . .

   a. to get help.

   b. to join the French army.

   c. because the English were attacking La Salle's fort.

   d. none of the above.

9. La Salle was killed by . . .

   a. his own men.

   b. the Karankawas.

   c. the Spanish.

   d. the flu.

10. Some of the things recovered from the *Belle* included . . .

    a. cannons.

    b. combs.

    c. a skeleton.

    d. all of the above.

Sequencing

Number the phrases in the sequence, or order, that they occur in the story.

_____ La Salle sails the *Belle* into Matagorda Bay.

_____ La Salle makes a plan to build a fort and attack Spanish forts and mines.

_____ La Salle and the colonists build a fort.

_____ Jean-Baptiste Talon is captured by Karankawas, and Pierre Talon is left with the Hasinai.

_____ A storm hits and the *Belle* sinks.

_____ The Talon brothers return to France.

_____ La Salle and 17 of his men go for help.

_____ Some of La Salle's men rebel and kill him.

_____ The Talon brothers are captured by Spanish patrols.

_____ La Salle sails for the New World with four ships and 300 men, women, and children.

Extension Activity

La Salle was just one of many explorers from France, Spain, and England to sail to the New World. In small groups of three or four, go to the library for information on New World explorers. Ask the librarian to help you locate books on people who explored the New World. Pick one explorer. Find at least three facts about this explorer and report them to your class.

Pre-reading Activities

Looking It Over

1. Read the title of the article that begins on page 58.

2. Leaf through the pages of the article, stopping to look at the illustrations.

3. Read the following list of vocabulary words.

Vocabulary

anthropologist   person who studies human physical development and culture.

Example: The anthropologist studied the tribe to find out why the members were so healthy.

forensic   used in legal matters

Example: An expert in forensic medicine testified in court.

rural   of, or related to, the countryside

Example: Mike was sick of the city and wanted to move to a rural area.

arthritis   swelling and pain in bone joints

Example: It was hard for Malcolm's mother to sew after she developed arthritis.

marrow   soft matter that fills the inside of bones

Example: The doctor cut open the bone to look at the marrow.

trauma   a wound or injury

Example: The dead body showed signs of trauma to the head.

Make a Prediction

What do you think this article will be about? Write your prediction and the reason you made it below.

Prediction _____

_____

_____

Reason _____

_____

_____

What do you know?

What do you know about skeletons? Make a list of everything you know or *think* you know about skeletons. Then read the article to add to your knowledge.

_____

_____

_____

_____

Bone Detective

Doug Owsley bends over a microscope. He is look- ing at bones, human bones. They could be the bones of a Native American who died from a fall 400 years ago. They could be from a white settler buried on a farm at the turn of the century. Or they could be the bones of a murder victim killed last year.

Owsley is a forensic anthropologist. He studies bones to learn about people. While he conducts historical research, bones tell him a lot. And he has a lot of questions. What did the person eat? Where and how did he or she live? What disease did he or she have? How long did the per- son live?

When the police come to him for help, they have their own set of questions. Who is this person? Was he or she murdered? If so, who did it? Sometimes the bones can give Owsley the answers.

The box on the floor contains a human skeleton. In Owsley's office it would be a surprise if the box held anything else. He already knows who the bones belonged to. A man wandered away from a nursing home. He was found dead in some nearby woods. The police want to know if the man simply got lost and died, or if someone killed him.

Most of Owsley's cases come from bones found in rural areas. A deer hunter stumbles across a skeleton. A dog digs up some old bones in a field. By the time this happens, bones are the only thing left. In the city, bodies are normally found soon after death. Body and clothing are somewhat intact so the police usually don't need an expert such as Owsley to help them solve the mystery.

Most of the time Owsley works with the police to solve crimes. However, he once had a case in which his work helped convict a police officer of murdering his girlfriend. He said he didn't have anything to do with it. Investigators found tiny bone chips in the back of the officer's truck.

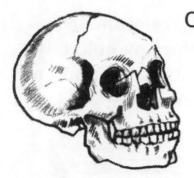

Owsley determined that the chips came from a human skull. "But it's the tiny traces of blood on the bone chips that helped nail him," says Owsley. The officer is now serving a life sentence, plus 20 years.

Owsley looks at the bones of the man from the nursing home. He can tell that the man had arthritis because some of the bones have ridges on the end. An envelope contains the man's hair. There is a lot of it, and it is dark. This indicates that the man was not old; he was only 45. His wife put him in the nursing home because he was losing his mind. The police think she may have been poisoning him.

Owsley cannot tell if the man has been poisoned just by looking at the bones. He sends a bone sample to another expert. The bone marrow will be examined for traces of poison. Owsley continues his investigation.

He studies each bone, looking for signs of trauma. The man's nose does not seem broken. A small bone in his throat is intact. This would indicate that the man probably was not choked. There are no cracks in his ribs or evidence that he was hit with something.

The bone marrow results come back. There was no trace of poisoning. Owsley has looked at each of the man's 205 bones. He has found no evidence of murder. But he is not finished. Owsley has a more powerful microscope down the hall. Tomorrow, he will begin the whole process over again.

Comprehension

Circle the best answer. Highlight the sentence or sentences in the story where you find the answer.

1. Doug Owsley studies . . .

   a. human bones.

   b. dog bones.

   c. whales.

   d. rivers.

2. By studying human bones, Owsley figures out . . .

   a. how long people lived.

   b. what people ate.

   c. which diseases people had.

   d. all of the above.

3. The police come to Owsley to find out . . .

   a. if a person was murdered.

   b. how much money a robber stole.

   c. the identity of a skeleton.

   d. a and c.

4. The man who wandered away from the nursing home was found dead . . .

   a. in a river.

   b. in a ditch.

   c. in a field.

   d. in the woods.

5. Most of Owsley's cases come from bones found . . .

   a. in the city.

   b. on top of mountains.

   c. in rural areas.

   d. under water.

6. Owsley helped convict a police officer who . . .

   a. killed his girlfriend.

   b. robbed a bank.

   c. sold drugs.

   d. none of the above.

7. Owsley could tell that the man from the nursing home had arthritis because . . .

   a. some of the bones had ridges on the end.

   b. the man's wife told him.

   c. a cane was found with the skeleton.

   d. medicine was found with the skeleton.

8. Police suspected the man's _____ of poisoning him.

   a. sister

   b. brother

   c. boss

   d. wife

9. Owsley had the bone marrow checked for . . .

   a. diseases.

   b. arthritis.

   c. traces of poison.

   d. none of the above.

10. After examining the body of the man from the nursing home, Owsley found . . .

   a. that the man had been poisoned.

   b. no evidence of murder.

   c. that the man had been shot.

   d. that the man had been strangled.

Inference

Bone Clues

Match each bone with the correct person clue.

Bone	Person
Bone A: Strange substance found in marrow.	_____ Person was a healthy adult.
Bone B: Rib bone is large and strong.	_____ Person was poisoned.
	_____ Person was strangled.
Bone C: Leg bones are broken.	_____ Person was a ballet dancer.
Bone D: Small bone in throat is crushed.	_____ Person was found at bottom of a cliff.
Bone E: Bones in feet show signs of hard use.	

Extension Activity

What do bones do? Find out. Go to the library for information on bones. Ask the librarian to help you locate books on bones. Look up bones in an encyclopedia. Find at least three facts about bones and report them to your class.

Pre-reading Activities

Looking It Over

1. Read the title of the article that begins on page 66.

2. Leaf through the pages of the article, stopping to look at the illustrations.

3. Read the following list of vocabulary words.

Vocabulary

matador a bullfighter

Example: The matador waved his cape in front of the bull.

opponent someone or something that is in conflict with another

Example: The matador's opponent is the bull.

hysterical to be very emotional

Example: Jason became hysterical when he saw the snake.

master to overcome or learn

Example: I hope to master hang-gliding after ten tries.

olé	used to express excited approval (Spanish)

Example: "¡Olé!" shouted the crowd after the Spanish figure skater landed a triple jump.

Make a Prediction

What do you think this article will be about? Write your prediction and the reason you made it below.

Prediction _____

_____

_____

Reason _____

_____

_____

What do you know?

What do you know about bull fighting? Make a list of everything you know or *think* you know about bullfighting. Then read the article to add to your knowledge.

_____

_____

_____

_____

_____

_____

¡Olé! Cristina

The bull stares at the matador across the dusty ring. Blood flows from cuts across its back and sides. The matador stares into the eyes of the bull. They are sizing each other up. Suddenly, the bull charges. The matador swings the cape in front of the bull like a windmill. The bull rushes past, barely missing the matador with its sharp horns. The bull is tired. The matador stands right in front of him and rubs his forehead with a small sword. It is time for the kill. The small sword is traded for the matador's longest, sharpest blade. Again, the bull thunders past the matador. The bull turns to face his opponent. The matador looks down the blade of the sword at the bull, almost like aiming a gun. The bull makes a last charge. Only one will leave the ring alive. Today, it will not be the bull!

When the fight is over, the crowd roars. Cries of "¡Olé! Cristina" fill the air. They are cheering Cristina Sánchez, Spain's most famous matadora and one of the few women to master the deadly sport.

Cristina grew up in Spain, watching her father fight bulls, but she did not follow in his footsteps immediately. Before Cristina became a matadora, she worked in a beauty parlor and as a typist. These jobs were not for her. Cristina likes to keep moving. She wanted a job that kept her on her toes. With a matador for a father, it is not surprising she looked to the bull ring for a career.

In 1996, when Cristina was 25, she earned the title *Matador de Toros* (Killer of Bulls). This means that you are an expert bullfighter. You have earned the right to fight the biggest, meanest bulls in the best rings.

Cristina is treated like a movie star. Crowds beg for her autograph. They shower her with gifts. At her fights, fans throw shoes, jackets, even crutches into the ring. She is so famous that a male matador made sure the rumor was spread that he and Cristina were in love. He was hoping that some of her fame would rub off on him.

However, some male matadors don't want to have anything to do with Cristina. They are upset that a woman would dare become a bullfighter. There are male matadors who refuse to fight in the same ring with Cristina. To protest this treatment, Cristina once fought six bulls in a row, instead of the usual two.

Some people have said that Cristina is too weak to make a good kill. At times, she does not push the sword in far enough, or she does not hit the exact right spot. However, many male matadors also have trouble with the final kill. Cristina says that strength is not as important as skill and experience.

Cristina is not the first female bullfighter. In 1940, Juanita Cruz became a matadora. In those days Juanita fought the bulls in a skirt instead of the tight pants that male matadors wore. Today, Cristina wears pants just like all the other matadors. The matador's uniform is called a *traje de luces* (suit of lights). It is very colorful and very expensive. Cristina owns some outfits that cost as much as $20,000. After each fight, a helper cleans it with soap and a toothbrush.

Most people would never dream of climbing into a ring with an animal that weighs up to a thousand pounds and has horns. Some have asked if anything scares Cristina. She says, " . . . people think that because I kill bulls I have to be really brave, but I'm not. I'm afraid of staying home by myself and I get hysterical if I see a spider."

Name _____

Comprehension

Circle the best answer. Highlight the sentence or sentences in the story where you find the answer.

1. Cristina Sánchez is one of Spain's most famous . . .

    a. rock stars.

    b. matadors.

    c. doctors.

    d. actors.

2. Cristina watched _____ fighting bulls as she grew up.

    a. her father

    b. her mother

    c. Juanita Cruz

    d. none of the above

3. Before Cristina became a matatodor, she worked . . .

    a. as a waitress.

    b. as a typist.

    c. in a beauty parlor.

    d. b and c.

4. When Cristina earned the title *Matador de Toros*, she was _____ years old.

    a. 12

    b. 17

    c. 25

    d. 20

5. In Spain, Cristina is treated . . .

    a. like a movie star.

    b. like a freak.

    c. like a criminal.

    d. none of the above.

6. Some male matadors won't fight in the same ring with Cristina because . . .

   a. they are afraid of her.

   b. she it too popular.

   c. they don't like her father.

   d. they don't think women should be bullfighters.

7. To protest her treatment by some male matadors Cristina . . .

   a. called them names.

   b. fought six bulls in a row.

   c. sued them.

   d. none of the above.

8. Cristina says that, for a matador, skill and experience . . .

   a. are more important than strength.

   b. are less important than strength.

   c. don't matter.

   d. b and c.

9. When Juanita Cruz fought bulls she wore . . .

   a. pants.

   b. a suit of armor.

   c. high heels.

   d. a skirt.

10. Cristina Sanchez is afraid of . . .

   a. snakes.

   b. staying home alone.

   c. spiders.

   d. b and c.

The Five Ws—Who, What, Where, When, Why

If you know the five Ws of an article, then you really understand it. Use complete sentences to fill in the five Ws of *¡Olé! Cristina*.

Who (Who is the article about?)

_____

What (What is the article about?)

_____

_____

Where (Where do the events in the article take place?)

_____

_____

When (When do the events in the article take place?)

_____

Why (Why is the article's subject important, interesting, or unusual?)

_____

_____

Extension Activity

Form a debate on the morality (right or wrong) of bullfighting. Divide into teams or debate in pairs these positions:

1. Bulls should not be killed for entertainment.

2. Some traditions are so important that they should continue, even when they offend some people.

Name _____

Pre-reading Activities

Looking It Over

1. Read the title of the article that begins on page 74.

2. Leaf through the pages of the article, stopping to look at the illustrations.

3. Read the following list of vocabulary words.

Vocabulary

hoax   something that tricks others

                                  Example: Some people think that Bigfoot is just a hoax.

dramatic   to be exciting

                                  Example: The launch of the first rocket to the moon was very dramatic.

mayhem   a period of destruction, confusion, and panic

                                  Example: The earthquake caused mayhem all over the city.

panic   sudden terror

                                  Example: There was panic in the camp when someone saw a bear.

script   written form of a play or movie

> **Example:** Actors have to study the script to learn their lines.

Make a Prediction

What do you think this article will be about? Write your prediction and the reason you made it below.

Prediction _____

_____

_____

Reason _____

_____

_____

What do you know?

What do you know about space aliens from Mars? Make a list of everything you know or *think* you know about space aliens from Mars. Then read the article to add to your knowledge.

_____

_____

_____

_____

_____

Alien Attack

It was the evening of October 30, 1938—the day before Halloween. Across the United States people fled from their homes in panic. Some dropped to their knees and prayed. Others ran screaming down the street. What caused this mayhem? Earth was under attack by an alien army from Mars.

That is what these people believed. Orson Welles chose that night to broadcast his version of H. G. Wells's novel *War of the Worlds.* The book is about an army from Mars attacking Earth. Orson Welles wanted to present *War of the Worlds* as a radio play. He had an idea of how to make it more dramatic than a normal play on the radio.

Welles's idea was to retell *War of the Worlds* with fake news broadcasts. Reports of an invading army from Mars that lands in New Jersey would be broadcast over the radio. The radio play's writer used a map of New Jersey to come up with the real names of towns and roads for the script. To pick the landing spot for the aliens he closed his eyes and stabbed the map with a pencil. It landed on Grovers Mill.

The night of the broadcast millions of people were listening to music on CBS's *Studio One.* Suddenly, a news bulletin interrupted the program. There was a report of gas explosions seen on the surface of Mars. A strange object had fallen from the skies near Grovers Mill, New Jersey. Scientists were on their way to check it out. Then the music returned.

Not much later, another report from Grovers Mill was broadcast. A humming metal object had landed in a farmer's field. Police and scientists were on the scene. The radio reporter described a scraping sound coming from inside the object. Then the end of the metal object began to turn like the lid of a jar.

Millions of people around the country heard the following report over their radios.

> Reporter: Ladies and gentlemen, this is the most terrifying thing I have ever witnessed! . . . Wait a minute! Someone's crawling out of the hollow top. Someone or . . . something.

The reporter went on to describe a horrible monster, as big as a bear, with gleaming eyes and saliva dripping from its mouth. Police walking toward the spaceship were torched by a heat ray. Across the United States, people thought these news reports were real.

Police stations were flooded with calls. People ran from their homes and wandered around in the streets. One woman was found in her bathroom holding a bottle of poison and screaming, "I'd rather die this way than like that!"

The mayor of a town in the Midwest reported mobs, violence, and looting.

Reports of more spaceships were broadcast. Most of New Jersey had been destroyed by the alien army. Black smoke was pouring across the state. In the real world, 20 families on one block rushed from their homes with wet cloths on their faces to protect themselves from the smoke.

News of the nationwide panic reached New York City. Police stormed the radio studio where Orson Welles was staging the play. During breaks in the show, an actor explained that the whole thing was a hoax. In fact, this had been said at the beginning of the show. But most listeners ignored, or did not hear, these messages. The panic continued.

The next day the program was headline news in papers across the country. Orson Welles and CBS were blamed for all of the trouble. Welles and the chairman of CBS said they were sorry for causing the panic.

Reporters wondered how so many people could be fooled by such a wild story. World War II was just around the corner. Did people's fear of the coming war make them more likely to believe reports of an attack from Mars? Or are people just willing to believe anything they hear or see, if it is presented as news?

Comprehension

Circle the best answer. Highlight the sentence or sentences in the story where you find the answer.

1. On October 30, 1938, people across the United States believed the country was being attacked by . . .

   a. Germany.

   b. Japan.

   c. Mars.

   d. Italy.

2. People believed the U. S. was under attack by aliens because . . .

   a. UFOs had really landed in New Jersey.

   b. fake newscasts of an attack were broadcast on the radio.

   c. people were dressing as space aliens for Halloween.

   d. fake newscasts of an attack were broadcast on television.

3. The play's writer picked the aliens' landing spot by . . .

   a. flipping a coin.

   b. asking Orson Welles.

   c. throwing a dart at a map of New Jersey.

   d. stabbing a map of New Jersey with a pencil.

4. The first news bulletin reported . . .

   a. gas explosions on Mars.

   b. aliens landing in Grovers Mill.

   c. aliens attacking New York City.

   d. none of the above.

5. Later news reports described . . .

   a. aliens crawling out of their space ship.

   b. aliens attacking the police with a heat ray.

   c. aliens destroying half of New Jersey.

   d. all of the above.

6. When people heard these news reports, they reacted by . . .

    a. calling the police.

    b. panicking.

    c. rushing into the streets.

    d. all of the above.

7. When news of the nationwide panic reached New York . . .

    a. police stormed the studio where the play was being staged.

    b. Orson Welles was arrested.

    c. an actor explained that the news reports were fake.

    d. a and c.

8. After the program was broadcast . . .

    a. Orson Welles and CBS were blamed for all of the trouble.

    b. Welles and the chairman of CBS said they were sorry.

    c. it was headline news across the country.

    d. all of the above.

9. Reporters wondered . . .

    a. how the army was able to defeat the aliens.

    b. how so many people could have been fooled.

    c. why Orson Welles was not arrested.

    d. when the aliens would return.

10. Orson Welles broadcast *War of the Worlds* . . .

    a. just before World War II.

    b. during World War II.

    c. just after World War II.

    d. in 1996.

Name _____

Write Your Own News Story

What if space aliens really did land on Earth? Write a news article describing the first landing of an alien space-ship. Remember to include the 5 Ws (Who, What, Where, When, Why) in your story. Use the space below for your notes. Write the final story on another sheet of paper.

_____

_____

_____

_____

_____

_____

_____

_____

Extension Activity

What do we know about Mars? What is the weather like? Is there life on Mars? Has there ever been life on Mars? Have humans ever landed on Mars? What does the surface of the planet look like? Find answers to these and other questions you may have. Look in science textbooks and try to find articles in magazines and newspapers. Conduct a search on the Internet using the key word *Mars* and see what you find. Report the results of your research to your class.

Answer Key

Anaconda

(Pages 10–11)

1. a	3. a	5. b	7. a	9. c
2. d	4. d	6. d	8. c	10. a

(Page 12)

1. soft	4. dark	7. big	10. small
2. squishy	5. young	8. flashy	
3. huge	6. small	9. unruly	

Tree Houses Grow Up

(Pages 19–20)

1. d	3. d	5. d	7. b	9. d
2. c	4. a	6. a	8. b	10. c

(Page 21)

1. grow	4. sell	7. tell	10. sleep
2. think	5. watch	8. bang	
3. build	6. put	9. look	

Bring 'Em Back Alive

(Pages 27–28)

1. a	3. c	5. d	7. c	9. b
2. c	4. d	6. d	8. a	10. c

(Page 29)

1. poodle	4. trainer	7. puppy	10. skin
2. snow	5. job	8. hero	
3. body	6. game	9. bunny	

The Enemy Within

(Pages 35–36)

1. c	3. a	5. b	7. a	9. b
2. d	4. b	6. d	8. d	10. c

(Page 37)

a, c, d—The Anasazi were under attack.
b, e, f—The Anasazi moved to join the Pueblo
    Indians' new religion.

Animal Hospital

(Pages 43–44)

1. d	3. c	5. d	7. b	9. a
2. b	4. a	6. b	8. a	10. d

Shipwrecked

(Pages 53–54)

1. c	3. d	5. b	7. d	9. a
2. a	4. a	6. c	8. a	10. d

(Page 55)

3
1
4
8
5
10
6
7
9
2

Bone Detective

(Pages 61–62)

1. a	3. d	5. c	7. a	9. c
2. d	4. d	6. a	8. d	10. b

(Page 63)

B
A
D
E
C

¡Olé! Cristina

(Pages 69–70)

1. b	3. d	5. a	7. b	9. d
2. a	4. c	6. d	8. a	10. d

Alien Attack

(Pages 77–78)

1. c	3. d	5. d	7. d	9. b
2. b	4. a	6. d	8. d	10. a